ATTENTION ADVERTISERS AND SPONSORS!

Capitol Times magazine is on the lookout for partners who share our commitment to truth and the promotion of Christian Conservative values. As a trusted publication in the United States, we strive to uphold the highest standards of journalism while championing principles that resonate with our readership.

By advertising with us, you not only gain access to our loyal audience but also align your brand with a publication that stands firm in its dedication to integrity and authenticity. Your support will enable us to continue delivering insightful content that informs, educates, and inspires.

Join us in our mission to make a difference in the world of media. Contact us today to explore advertising and sponsorship opportunities with Capitol Times magazine. Together, let's amplify the voice of conservatism and uphold the values that matter most.

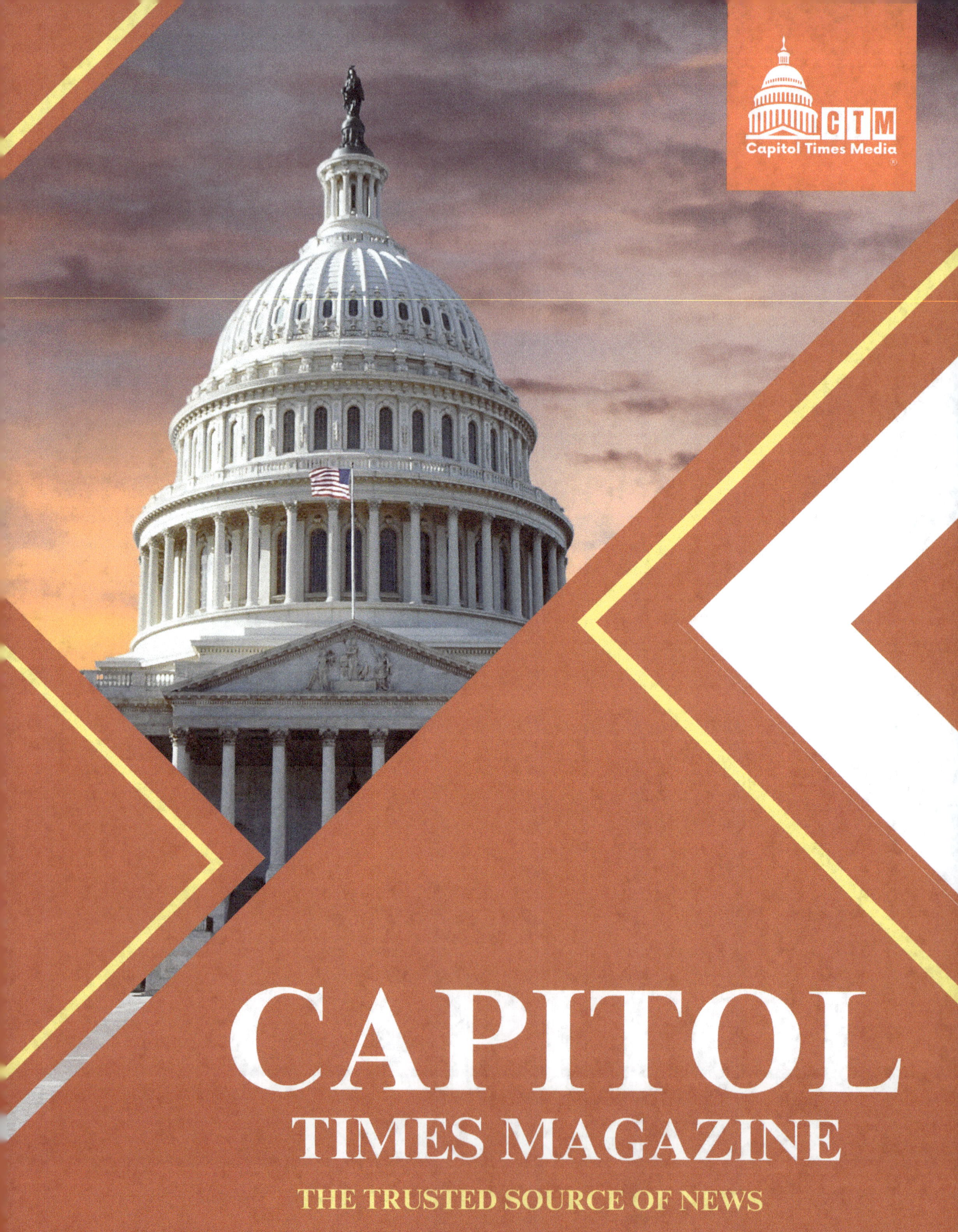

CTM
Capitol Times Media
CAPITOL
TIMES MAGAZINE
THE TRUSTED SOURCE OF NEWS

Will you be prepared? Experts in their fields including law enforcement and high level security experts will spend an extensive and intensive hands on training day with you!

Go to: www.WFFA.win
Become a participant in the fight to save freedom
- be prepared for 2024.

For Tickets and More Info www.meet4america.org

Help us eradicate the Evils of Child Sex Trafficking

"There is an unseen evil in this world, it has no prejudice nor does it see color, economic status or gender, it is called human trafficking. After being on the frontlines and witnessing these unspeakable horrific acts you can never be the same. Our organization will not rest until we put an end to this evil."
~ Christie Hutcherson, Founder/President

https://givesendgo/WFFABorder
Learn more at WFFA.win

A PAC to Save America

"We have real enemies, dedicated to dominating and eventually destroying us, and they are not going to be talked out of their hatred".

"We will be unapologetic for standing up for American values and principles. America does not back down from anyone or anything."

TEXT: FLYNN 91776

"We are fundamentally responsible for securing the future of our people and we can pursue this goal boldly in the knowledge that doing so has the derivative effect of improving the lives of people around the globe."

Local Action results in National Impact but only if we make the decision to be courageous for our families, our communities and our country.
The time to stand up, step up and speak up is now.

Paid for by Fight Like A Flynn (www.fightlikeaflynnpac.com). Not authorized by any candidate or candidate's committee

Support us at: www.FightLikeAFlynnPAC.com

Freedom
FORUM

MON - THUR - FRI
8:00 pm EST
www.capitoltimesmedia.com
HOSTED BY DAVID COLBERT
LIVE
STREAMING

f
LIVE

LISTEN ON SPOTIFY

JOHN 6:35. JESUS SAID, "I AM THE BREAD OF LIFE; WHOEVER COMES TO ME SHALL NOT HUNGER, AND WHOEVER BELIEVES IN ME SHALL NEVER THIRST." ...

Capitol Times

Magazine

www.capitoltimesmedia.com

Editor-In-Chief
Anil Anwar

Publisher
Capitol Times Media

Magazine Graphic design
Sandra Clarke

Front Cover
Photo Source/Provided By:
Jonathan

Capitol Times Magazine

Owned by Capitol Times Media
Printed in the United States of America
©All Rights Reserved - 2024

www.capitoltimesmedia.com
editor@capitoltimesmedia.com

Copyright Disclaimer: Capitol Times Magazine utilizes photos solely for editorial purposes and provides proper credit to the copyright holders.

Disclaimer

The views and opinions expressed in the articles or Interviews published in this magazine are solely those of the respective authors and do not necessarily reflect the official policy or position of the Capitol Times magazine, its editors, or its staff. The authors are solely responsible for the content of their articles.

The magazine strives to provide a platform for diverse voices and opinions, and we value the principle of free expression.

The magazine assumes no responsibility or liability for any errors or omissions in the content of the articles. In no event shall the Capitol Times magazine be liable for any special, direct, indirect, or incidental damages.

Furthermore, the inclusion of advertisements or sponsored content in Capitol Times magazine does not constitute an endorsement or guarantee of the products, services, or views promoted by the advertisers. Readers are encouraged to conduct their own research and exercise caution when making decisions based on advertisements or sponsored content featured in this publication.

Thank you for reading and engaging with our publication. Your feedback is valuable to us as we continue to provide a platform for thought-provoking content and diverse perspectives.

Review Rating

Thomas S

A must read. Turn off the TV. Sit down and read this. Then read it again.

Julie B

All Americans MUST read! This story is amazing and one every American must know.

Leslie D Keller

Important and great article on Patrick Byrne. Everybody needs to read this.

Review Rating

Martha Boneta

Excellent Magazine featuring
Patrick Byrne.
Exceptional journalism and cover
story featuring Patrick Byrne!

★★★★★

David Colbert

A Riveting Read: Capitol Times
Magazine Unveils the Truth about
the Deep State

★★★★★

It reveals shocking details about our intelligence
agencies, our election system, and how our intelligence
community seeks successful and powerful resources
from the private sector to help them achieve
objectives. America is in peril from foreign enemies and
we must peacefully unite if we want to save our
country. Time is running short for us to be successful.

★★★★★

Anil Anwar
Editor-in-Chief

Editor's Note

Welcome to the latest issue of Capitol Times Magazine, your trusted source for conservative news and insightful political analysis in the United States. As we embark on another edition filled with thought-provoking articles and in-depth coverage, we are proud to reaffirm our commitment to delivering high-quality journalism that resonates with our readership.

At Capitol Times, we understand the importance of providing a platform for diverse perspectives and robust debate, and this issue is no exception. Packed with a myriad of informative political articles, our team has worked tirelessly to bring you a comprehensive overview of the current landscape, offering insights that are both enlightening and impactful.

As you delve into the pages of this issue, we encourage you to engage critically with the content, challenging your own perspectives and embracing the opportunity to broaden your understanding of the issues at hand. Whether you're a seasoned political aficionado or just beginning to explore the intricacies of governance, there is something within these pages to captivate and inform.

We would like to extend our sincerest gratitude to our dedicated team of writers, editors, and contributors who have poured their passion and expertise into making this issue possible. Their unwavering commitment to excellence is evident in every word, and we are incredibly grateful for their tireless efforts.

To our readers, we thank you for your continued support and trust in Capitol Times Magazine. It is truly an honor to serve as your go-to source for conservative news and analysis, and we look forward to continuing this journey together.

CAPITOL TIMES MAGAZINE

CONTENTS

07 ISSUE

FEBRUARY | 2024

www.capitoltimesmedia.com

EXCLUSIVE!

Interview with

15

A DEEP DIVE INTO US POLITICS WITH JONATHAN

editor@capitoltimesmeidia.com

www.capitoltimesmedia.com

Stay Informed with Capitol Times Magazine!

Your Ultimate Source for US National News, Right in the Heart of Capitol.
Grab Your Copy Today and Stay Ahead of the Times!

A PAC to Save America

"We have real enemies, dedicated to dominating and eventually destroying us, and they are not going to be talked out of their hatred".

"We will be unapologetic for standing up for American values and principles. America does not back down from anyone or anything."

TEXT: FLYNN 91776

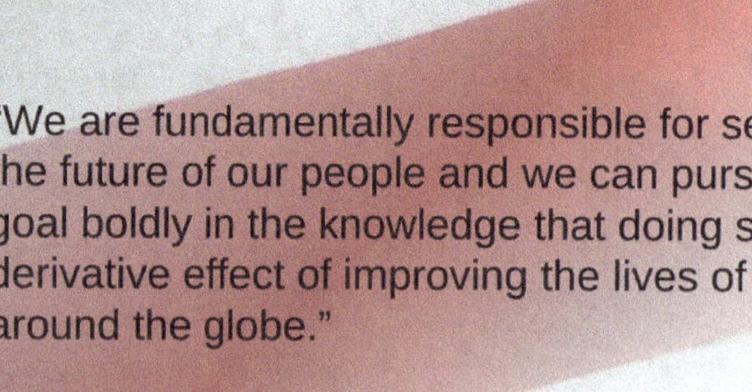

"We are fundamentally responsible for securing the future of our people and we can pursue this goal boldly in the knowledge that doing so has the derivative effect of improving the lives of people around the globe."

Local Action results in National Impact but only if we make the decision to be courageous for our families, our communities and our country.
The time to stand up, step up and speak up is now.

Paid for by Fight Like A Flynn (www.fightlikeaflynnpac.com). Not authorized by any candidate or candidate's committee

Support us at: www.FightLikeAFlynnPAC.com

A Deep Dive into US
Politics with Jonathan

ANIL: Jonathan, there's been significant controversy surrounding Adam Schiff's proposal to end the Electoral College. What are your thoughts on how such a move might impact the democratic process, and do you believe it could lead to more or less representative outcomes in future elections?

JONATHAN: I think ending the electoral college is a terrible idea that can never be allowed to happen, especially considering the current border invasion that is happening right now as well as the amount of representation of states in Congress based upon population, which can also be massively influenced by cheating in a few select sizable metro areas. The framers understood this and developed the electoral college as a check and balance against the potential of our republic ever devolving into a pure democracy. The areas with some of the most election corruption in the world, like New York City, Los Angeles, Chicago, Illinois, Fulton County, Georgia, and Harris County, Texas, could then just leverage their massive election fraud operations to impact not only the presidential popular vote but also the number of delegates those states get in Congress. So it becomes a vicious cycle that only continues to feed itself with each new stolen election.

ANIL: In light of Hunter Biden's recent decision to volunteer for testimony before Congress, how do you perceive this change of stance, especially considering the looming contempt of Congress citation? What impact, if any, do you think this might have on the ongoing investigation into Joe Biden, and how does it reflect on the broader issues raised about the Biden family's alleged influence peddling?

JONATHAN: Considering what we know about Hunter Biden, the FBI, Merrick Garland, and the DOJ under the current administration, if Hunter Biden is volunteering to testify, it's because they have a plan to enter into the record what they want on the record. They would then leverage those on-record facts as a protective layer of selective prosecution, and under the guise of an "ongoing investigation," the DOJ could insulate him from the investigation or prosecution of his more serious crimes with broader implications.

ANIL: Trump's second term agenda to "thoroughly drain the swamp." As a conservative activist, what specific policies or actions do you believe would constitute this agenda, and how do you think it aligns with the principles of the conservative movement? Additionally, what are your thoughts on the perception that such an agenda might evoke fear among those on the Left?

JONATHAN: To truly drain the swamp, it's going to take election integrity (first and foremost) everywhere and the defense of our borders. For Trump to have a successful administration and actually bring Washington, DC, to heel, those two agendas must be the primary directives. Mass deportations and criminal prosecution for both election crimes and coordinated illegal immigration efforts must happen as well. We must also address the elephant in the room and finally hold Israel and China accountable for their involvement in both the stealing of our elections and the creation and release of COVID upon the world.

ANIL: Trump's second term agenda has the Left feeling uneasy. In your opinion, what elements of Trump's proposed agenda might be causing this reaction, and how do you think conservatives can engage in meaningful discussions to address concerns and bridge the ideological divide? Additionally, how can the conservative movement work towards effective governance while navigating these differing perspectives?

JONATHAN: I feel like a lot of the Left's agenda centers around coordinated efforts of globalization, psychological manipulation, and years of psychological programming (propagandizing) by intelligence agencies, foreign operators, and corporate interests.

Many of the so-called "agendas" they have are not at all organic. But rather, well-funded subversion half truths or total falsehoods, with an overall goal of undermining millions of regular American Democrats and Republicans alike. The invasion at our border is a perfect example of this. It's designed to dilute America with millions of foreigners who have no allegiance to our country or our values, make our neighborhoods less safe, and have the ultimate goal of ruining the middle class via added taxation designed to fund support programs for these same illegal immigrants.

The conservative movement would be wise to focus on the bipartisanship of the problem we face. We must focus on both the constitutional mandates of the federal government to protect and defend our borders, while also reminding our counterparts across the aisle that these invaders will find their way to everyone's neighborhoods and backyards.

ANIL: Joe Biden's unfavorable standing in polls, being referred to as the "worst president in American history." How do you interpret these poll numbers, and in your opinion, what specific aspects of Biden's presidency contribute to this widespread perception? How might these poll results impact conservative messaging and strategies leading up to the next election?

JONATHAN: Biden is certainly the worst president in my lifetime, and I'm not surprised to see his poll numbers so low as a result. In fact, they're probably much worse than even what's portrayed in our manipulated polling systems. But it certainly makes sense when you realize he's operating on behalf of corporations and foreign interests while trying to protect his cronies (and his son) instead of working on behalf of the American people first and foremost.

I'm of the belief that middle America will decide the next election, assuming we can get some semblance of election integrity in the key areas across the country. It's not rocket science to look around and see if the jobs aren't there; gas prices are too high, and you have an administration more concerned with defending the borders of Israel in Ukraine. And they are defending our own borders. And most people aren't stupid; they can clearly see that it's likely the current administration is actively supporting the ongoing border invasion, and they want it to continue. It's just not sustainable for America, and again, it shouldn't be a partisan issue.

ANIL: Biden's "crooked business dealings" not fully coming to light. As a conservative activist, what information or evidence do you believe supports these claims, and how might the revelation of such details affect public trust in the Biden administration? In your view, what role should the media play in investigating and reporting on these allegations?

JONATHAN: I think we've only scratched the surface of how bad Biden and his family's business dealings really are on the corruption scale. The DOJ, the intelligence agencies, and most other federal agencies have been handpicked by Biden and his cronies for a reason. And if you paid attention at all to the law, fair against President Trump, it's pretty clear that our current court system, or federal law enforcement agencies, and our intelligence agencies are only interested in destroying Biden's enemies in protecting his (and their) interests.

Things are going to get much worse in 2024 before they get better, considering all of the information that's currently coming out and that will continue to pour out in the first and second quarters of this year.

ANIL: How do you think conservative media can influence public perceptions, especially considering the media landscape's perceived biases? What role do you believe conservative outlets should play in shaping the narrative around Biden's presidency and potential impeachment?

JONATHAN: I think conservative media will have to work harder than they've ever worked, and I believe they have an obligation to the American people and to the country to shine a light on everything that's currently happening both here and abroad. I got involved with investigative work and intelligence gathering work because I felt betrayed and let down by most major, conservative "talking heads" and media outlets.

I've given my life to this work because I know the situation that we face is grave, and the faith of the country hangs in the balance. Conservative media would be well served to stop focusing on the ancillary issues or the symptoms and instead turn their attention to the heart of what's causing each of those issues.

ANIL: Vivek Ramaswamy recently suspended his presidential campaign following the Iowa Caucuses and endorsed Donald Trump. How do you interpret this decision, and what implications do you think it has for the broader conservative movement? In your view, how might Ramaswamy's endorsement influence the dynamics of the Republican primary race?

JONATHAN: I think it was the 100% correct move by Vivek. And even though he still has a ways to go to fully earn my trust, he absolutely did the right thing here, in my opinion.

ANIL: With Ramaswamy endorsing Trump and emphasizing the need for an "America-First" candidate in the White House, what do you see as the future of America-first leadership within the conservative movement? How can conservatives build on this momentum to ensure the principles of putting America first remain central to the party's vision and policy goals?

JONATHAN: Americans are fed up with bills being passed in secret, at the last minute, and without sufficient time for them to be read. And they are sick and tired of seeing congressmen and women basically extorting each other into signing bills that are favorable to foreign interests, just so they'll agree to doing their duties to the American people. This must stop.

Americans are tired of seeing us get into wars to enrich a select few. We would prefer that America's leaders turn all of their attention for the foreseeable future towards restoring America and getting our own house in order before choosing to send billions of dollars to support the pensions, the borders, and the defenses of foreign (and corrupt) nations that largely don't share our nation's values.

ANIL: Donald Trump has decisively won the 2024 Republican presidential primary with a significant lead over Governor DeSantis and Ambassador Haley. How do you interpret Trump's dominance in this early stage of the primary, and what factors do you think contributed to his strong performance? In your view, what does this mean for the direction of the Republican Party?

JONATHAN: More so than any other candidate, I think Donald Trump represents someone who can't be bought, who focuses on what's best for America before any other country, and they can clearly see that he is public enemy number one of the deep state. I'm reminded of the old adage, "The enemy of my enemy is my friend."

Even people who only halfway pay attention to politics or world issues can understand this analogy and realize that Washington, DC, most fears what they can't control. And that's Donald Trump.

ANIL: Trump won over Evangelical voters, a group that Governor DeSantis actively courted. What do you think influenced Evangelicals to overwhelmingly support Trump, and how might this impact DeSantis' campaign strategy moving forward? How significant is the Evangelical vote in shaping the overall conservative landscape?

JONATHAN: In my opinion DeSantis's biggest mistake was surrounding himself with people who have a history of undermining Judeo-Christian conservatives, whether it be evangelical, Catholic, or protestant Christians, or our friends in the orthodox Jewish community.

Each of these faiths is built upon truth, love, righteousness, and a fear of our Creator, who calls upon us to demonstrate our love and service of Him by how we live our lives and interact with our fellow man.

ANIL: illegal immigration and border crisis as a key issue that steered the Iowa Caucuses. From a conservative perspective, how do you see this issue resonating with voters, and how might it shape the national conversation on immigration leading up to the 2024 election? What policy proposals do you believe resonate most strongly with voters concerned about the border crisis?

JONATHAN: I've mostly touched on this already, but it is by far the number one issue with voters in the 2024 election. That's largely because it puts the taxpayer in danger in two different ways: the destruction of the middle class through taxation and the endangerment of our families due to the infiltration of undocumented (potentially violent) border crossers.

At this point, we have no choice but to do each of the following:

1. Close the border.
2. Enforce current laws on the books.
3. Mass deportation of illegal immigrants.

ANIL: Trump's substantial lead in the primary may indicate a strong base of support, but it also suggests potential divisions within the party. How can conservatives navigate these dynamics to ensure a unified front heading into the general election? Do you see any challenges or opportunities for building consensus within the Republican Party based on the primary results?

JONATHAN: I think there's more consensus within the party then there is division. They always say to follow the money, and Nikki Haley is funded by the same people who supported Hillary Clinton. Reid Hoffman is one of those prominent financiers. Haley and DeSantis are/were both Democrats, in my opinion, simply based on the company they keep and the big money behind them.

ANIL: The issues that influenced the Iowa Caucuses, such as immigration and border security, what do you believe are the key priorities for conservatives in the 2024 election? How can conservative candidates effectively address these concerns and present a compelling vision for the future, especially in the context of a highly competitive primary season?

JONATHAN:

1. Border Security.
2. Restoring jobs here at home.
3. No more money for Ukraine or Israel before America is taken care of.
4. Protect children at all costs.
5. Investigate, prosecute, and attain justice for the creation, release, and coverup of COVID.

Thank you, Anil.

ANIL: You are Welcome, and Thank you so much Jonathan

Advertisement

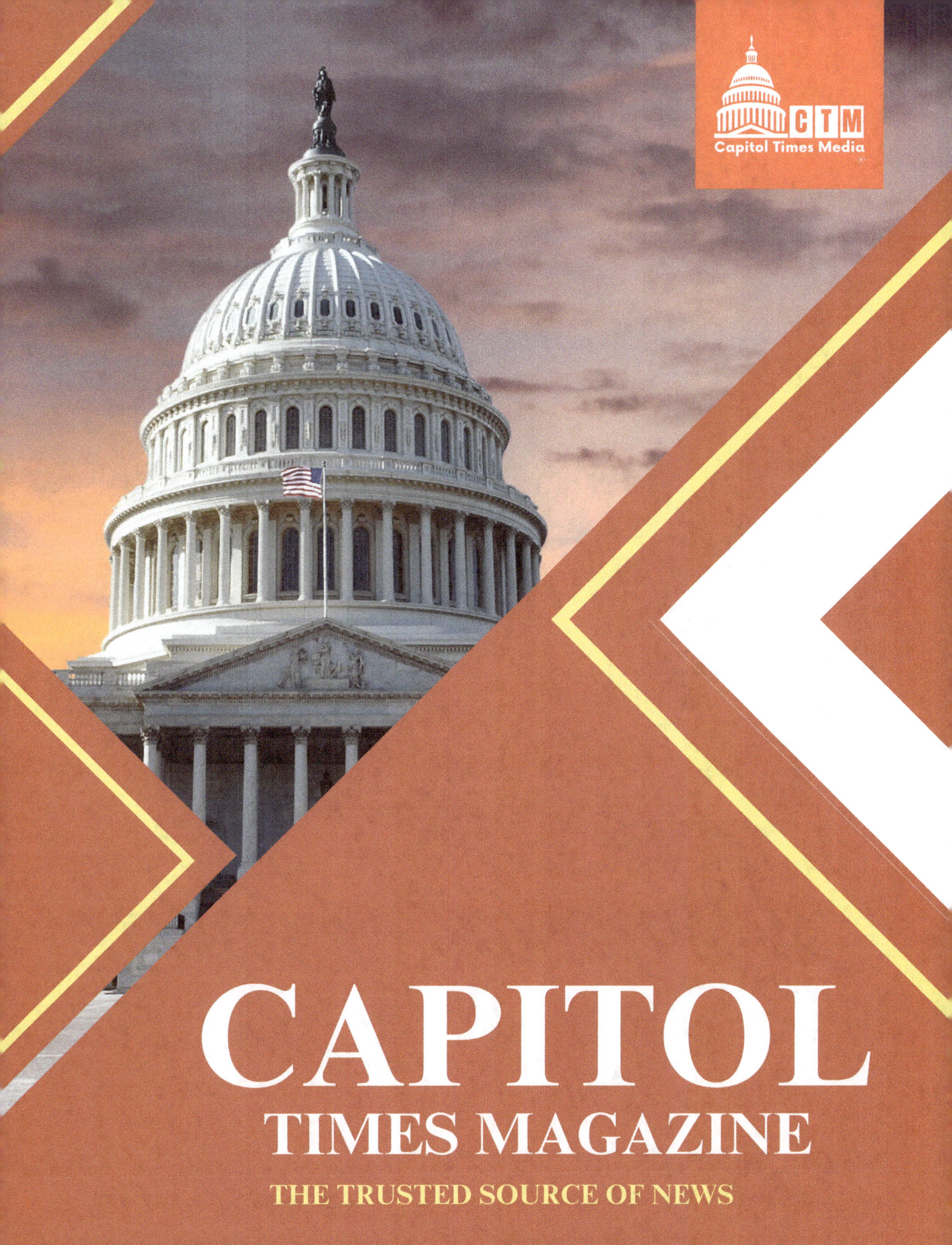

CTM
Capitol Times Media

CAPITOL
TIMES MAGAZINE
THE TRUSTED SOURCE OF NEWS

Studiodragonfly 19®

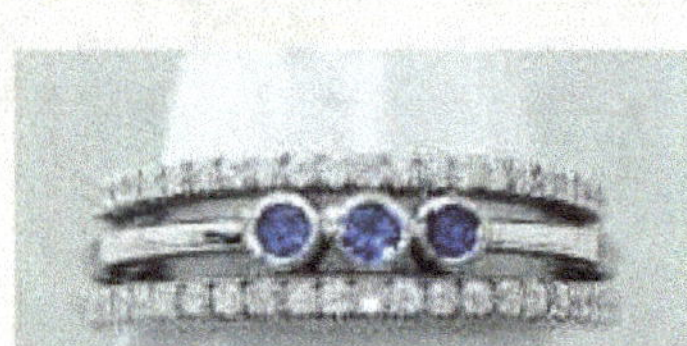

Memorial Jewelry

Marla B. Lindner
Owner / Designer

612.702.5605
Marlabethliss@gmail.com

Studiodragonfly19.com
Studiodragonfly19.etsy.com

BIDEN'S UNPREDICTABLE
Role in the China Equation

President Biden met with President Xi of the PRC before the 2022 G20 Bali Summit. PHOTO: White House

As the political landscape gears up for the 2024 presidential contest, one looming specter casts a shadow of uncertainty over the Biden administration: China. Unlike the predictable rhythms of the economy, China presents a complex and volatile wildcard that could significantly impact the outcome of the upcoming election. Traditionally, the economy has been the paramount factor in presidential elections, as famously underscored by the Clinton campaign's mantra, "It's the economy, stupid." Yet, in 2024, the economic landscape appears relatively stable, with inflation under control and the economy maintaining a steady course. While important, it lacks the volatility and potential for dramatic shifts that typically drive electoral outcomes.

In contrast, China emerges as a dynamic and unpredictable force on the political stage. As the world's second-largest economy and America's chief global adversary, China holds immense importance for both policymakers and the American people. However, its trajectory is far from certain, making it a potent wildcard in the presidential contest.

The internal and external challenges facing China are myriad, largely of its own making, and have the potential to render the nation highly volatile. This volatility extends not only to China's actions on the world stage but also to its role as a pivotal political factor in the upcoming election.

President Biden finds himself uniquely susceptible on the issue of China. His administration's approach to handling China's rise has drawn scrutiny from both ends of the political spectrum, with critics alleging weakness in the face of Beijing's aggression and human rights abuses.

Moreover, the evolving dynamics within China itself add another layer of uncertainty to the equation. As the regime grapples with domestic challenges and seeks to assert its global influence, the potential for unforeseen disruptions looms large.

The confluence of these factors underscores the great importance, great uncertainty, and great vulnerability that China represents for the Biden administration in 2024. While the economy may be largely "set" in the eyes of voters, China remains a fluid and dynamic variable that could fundamentally reshape the political landscape.

As the election cycle unfolds, candidates and voters alike will grapple with the implications of China's role in shaping America's future. How President Biden navigates these challenges and addresses the concerns of the American people on this critical issue will undoubtedly play a pivotal role in determining the outcome of the 2024 election.

In recent years, China's meteoric rise on the economic stage has captivated the world's attention. However, beneath the facade of a booming economy lies a troubling reality: China's economic strength is built on shaky foundations, and its aggressive foreign policy poses a growing threat to global stability.

While China boasts a massive economy, fueled by borrowing-financed spending on infrastructure and real estate, this growth has led to the creation of dangerous bubbles. The COVID-19 pandemic dealt a severe blow to China's economy, resulting in a prolonged national shutdown from which recovery remains elusive. Despite promises of economic reforms, state intervention has only deepened, stifling much-needed progress. Furthermore, foreign direct investment in China has slowed, with some quarters even showing negative growth. Chinese consumer spending continues to lag behind expectations, further exacerbating economic woes.

Compounding these internal challenges is China's increasingly assertive foreign policy. From aggressive moves against neighboring countries like India, Taiwan, and Japan, to broader displays of belligerence across Asia and the Pacific, China's actions have raised alarms worldwide. Notably, China's alliances with rogue regimes like Russia, Iran, and North Korea underscore its willingness to align with global troublemakers.

The convergence of internal instability and external aggression presents a potent cocktail of risks for the international community. China's predatory business practices at home and abroad, coupled with its support for Russia in conflicts like the Ukrainian invasion, demonstrate the potential for volatility on a global scale. These challenges have not gone unnoticed by the Biden administration, which has grappled with China's increasingly assertive behavior. From diplomatic spats to security concerns, China's actions have created headaches for US policymakers, with the potential for even greater disruptions as the next election cycle approaches.

China's outward image of economic strength and global influence belies a fragile reality. As internal problems mount and external aggression persists, the world must remain vigilant in addressing the challenges posed by China's rise. Failure to do so risks further destabilization and conflict in an already precarious global landscape.

In the ever-evolving landscape of US politics, one theme remains constant: the specter of China looms large, casting a shadow of concern and scrutiny over policymakers and leaders alike. As the Biden administration navigates its course, the echoes of past statements and actions reverberate, inviting a critical examination of its approach to the rising global power.

During his 2019 campaign in Iowa, President Biden's remarks regarding China sparked widespread controversy and raised eyebrows across the political spectrum. His assertion that "China is going to eat our lunch" was swiftly followed by a seemingly conciliatory tone, suggesting that China posed no real competition to the United States. However, such sentiments were met with rightful skepticism and outcry, prompting Republicans to seize upon these remarks as a rallying cry against Biden's perceived naivety and weakness on the international stage.

Indeed, Republicans have not shied away from reminding the American public of Biden's statements, utilizing them as potent ammunition in their ongoing critique of his administration's approach to China. From questioning the administration's communication with Chinese officials during the COVID-19 pandemic to alleging a downplaying of China's role in the global crisis, Republicans have made it clear that they will not let Biden off the hook easily.

Furthermore, the issue of climate change has emerged as a contentious point of contention in the Biden-China discourse. While Republicans accuse the administration of being too lenient on China due to its climate agenda, environmental advocates express dismay over China's lack of cooperation on this front. The clash between environmental priorities and geopolitical realities underscores the complexity of US-China relations and the challenges facing the Biden administration in balancing competing interests.

Central to the conservative critique of Biden's approach to China are questions surrounding personal involvement and potential conflicts of interest. The repeated invocation of Hunter Biden's business dealings in China, coupled with scrutiny of Joe Biden's role in these affairs, serves as a potent reminder of the ethical challenges facing the administration. Republicans are poised to leverage these issues as part of their broader narrative of Democratic hypocrisy and cronyism.

As the political landscape continues to evolve, one thing remains clear: the specter of China will continue to shape the contours of US politics, driving debate and scrutiny at every turn. For the Biden administration, navigating these treacherous waters requires a delicate balancing act, one that acknowledges the complexities of US-China relations while upholding American values and interests. In the face of relentless Republican scrutiny, the true test lies in whether the administration can rise to the challenge and chart a course that safeguards America's interests in an increasingly uncertain world.

Few issues possess the potency to unite disparate factions quite like the looming shadow of China. Regardless of party affiliation, there is a resounding consensus: China's significance is undeniable, and its actions are met with widespread disdain. As the political landscape evolves, China's stature parallels that of the economy, with its influence shaping policy agendas and driving electoral dynamics. Yet, where the economy provides a stable foundation, China's unpredictability injects an element of volatility into the equation.

In recent years, China has emerged as a rogue nation, flaunting international norms and charting its own course with scant regard for stability or predictability. This renegade behavior underscores the urgency of addressing China's ascendance as a global power and the challenges it poses to American interests.

While sentiments toward China may be entrenched, the role it will play in shaping the political fortunes of President Joe Biden remains uncertain. The looming question is whether China will emerge as a formidable adversary, leveraging its influence to undermine Biden's agenda, or serve as a rallying point for bipartisan opposition.

For Republicans, China presents a strategic opportunity to challenge Biden's leadership and exploit perceived vulnerabilities on the international stage. With tensions simmering over trade, human rights abuses, and geopolitical maneuvering, Republicans are poised to harness anti-China sentiment to their advantage, casting Biden as weak on national security and beholden to foreign interests.

Indeed, China stands as Biden's most formidable wild card heading into the 2024 election cycle. How he navigates the complex terrain of U.S.-China relations will undoubtedly shape his legacy and determine his political fortunes. The stakes could not be higher, as the outcome will reverberate far beyond the confines of partisan politics, impacting America's standing on the world stage and the trajectory of global affairs.

As the Biden administration grapples with the challenges posed by an assertive China, it must remain vigilant and resolute in defending American interests and values. Whether China emerges as a foil or a formidable adversary, one thing is clear: the road ahead will be fraught with uncertainty, and the stakes could not be higher. In the high-stakes game of geopolitics, navigating the China conundrum will require deft diplomacy, unwavering resolve, and a clear-eyed assessment of America's interests.

EXCLUSIVE INVITATION

The Honor of Your Presence is Requested at a

BORDER911 Gala

501(C)(3) Foundation

The **Mar-a-Lago** Club

Poolside Reception

Formal Gala Dinner in Ballroom

Dignitaries, Members
of Congress and Celebrities

Kash Patel

Sebastian Gorka
EMCEE

The Honorable

Tom Homan

Former ICE Director to the 45th President, Donald J. Trump

BORDER 911 Team

Sara Carter | Mark Morgan | Derek Maltz | Rodney Scott | Jaeson Jones

Host Committee

Matt Whitaker | Anthony Marlowe | Steve Moore | Sam Sorbo
Kevin Sorbo | Monica Crowley | Joe Piscopo | Congressman Ronny Jackson

April 4, 2024

BORDER911.com/events/

6:00PM - Poolside Reception
7:30PM - Ballroom Gala
Black Tie

Do Not Miss This Historic Once In A Lifetime Extravaganza!

Poolside Reception $ 900
Gala and Reception $ 2,500
Maga Patriot $ 10,000
(Private round table with celebrity)

Ambassador $ 5,000
(Includes Red Carpet Pictures
and VIP seating)

Sponsor $ 100,000

Text: Martha 571 839 1143

Donations submitted through donation forms on this site are tax-deductible to the extent allowed by law and are proccessed in U.S. dollars. BORDER911 Foundation, Inc. is a U.S. nonprofit, tax-exempt charitable organization (Tax Identification Number 93-3033002) under Section 501(c)(3) of the U.S. Internal Revenue Code.

HEALTH INSURANCE COVERAGE EXTENDED TO

1 MILLION

ILLEGAL MIGRANTS

In a troubling revelation, NPR has shed light on a disturbing trend: the provision of full health insurance coverage to over 1 million low-income immigrants, regardless of their legal status, across eleven states and Washington, D.C. This startling revelation underscores the growing burden placed on American taxpayers and the erosion of immigration law enforcement.

The justification provided for extending health insurance coverage to illegal migrants is particularly alarming. According to the report, hospitals have voiced complaints about the financial strain of providing medical treatment to undocumented individuals without insurance. This has led to the implementation of state-funded health insurance programs, effectively rewarding illegal immigration and incentivizing further unlawful entry into the United States.

At the heart of this issue lies the program known as Emergency Medicaid, wherein states reimburse hospitals for providing emergency medical services to unauthorized residents. While originally intended to address immediate healthcare needs in emergency situations, this program has morphed into a vehicle for extending benefits far beyond its intended scope. Moreover, the expansion of coverage to include prenatal care in some states further illustrates the erosion of legal boundaries and the normalization of benefits for illegal immigrants.

The implications of providing full state-provided health insurance coverage to illegal migrants are profound. Not only does it strain already overburdened healthcare systems and strain taxpayer resources, but it also serves as a magnet for individuals from around the world seeking to exploit America's generosity.

By extending such benefits, policymakers are effectively signaling that illegal immigration will be rewarded rather than deterred, perpetuating a cycle of lawlessness and dependency.

Furthermore, the moral hazard inherent in providing taxpayer-funded benefits to individuals who have circumvented the legal immigration process cannot be overstated. It undermines the integrity of the immigration system, diminishes respect for the rule of law, and sends a message that illegal behavior will be tolerated and even rewarded.

As conservative voices, it is imperative that we staunchly oppose the normalization of benefits for illegal immigrants and advocate for the enforcement of immigration laws.

We must demand accountability from elected officials and insist on policies that prioritize the interests of American citizens and lawful residents. The provision of taxpayer-funded health coverage to illegal migrants is not only fiscally irresponsible but morally reprehensible, and it is high time for decisive action to address this egregious misuse of taxpayer resources.

California's latest move to extend health care benefits to illegal migrants is a blatant disregard for the rule of law and a dangerous precedent that threatens to exacerbate the ongoing crisis at the southern border.

Starting January 1, 2024, illegal migrants will be eligible for coverage under Medi-Cal, the state's Medicaid program, effectively rewarding lawlessness and incentivizing further illegal immigration.

The expansion of Medi-Cal to include an estimated 700,000 illegal migrants between the ages of 26 and 49 is a staggering concession to individuals who have flouted immigration laws and entered the country illegally. This decision not only strains taxpayer resources but also undermines efforts to secure the border and enforce immigration laws.

A recent post from U.S. Customs and Border Protection underscores the gravity of the situation. Despite the majority of illegal migrants being ineligible to stay in the U.S. under asylum laws, the promise of health care and other benefits serves as a powerful incentive for individuals to take the risk and enter the country illegally. With over 2.4 million encounters in fiscal year 2023 and approximately 700,000 illegal crossings recorded through December of fiscal 2024, the border crisis shows no signs of abating.

Despite mounting complaints from blue city mayors and local officials overwhelmed by the influx of illegal migrants, President Biden remains obstinately indifferent to their concerns. His failure to address the root causes of the crisis and enact meaningful immigration reform only serves to embolden illegal migrants and perpetuate the cycle of lawlessness.

Moreover, Biden's approach mirrors that of his predecessor, former President Obama, who was similarly fixated on fundamentally transforming the United States. By prioritizing the interests of illegal migrants over those of American citizens and lawful residents, Biden and his administration continue to erode the fabric of our nation and undermine the principles of sovereignty and the rule of law.

As conservatives, it is incumbent upon us to staunchly oppose California's reckless disregard for immigration laws and demand accountability from elected officials. The provision of health care benefits to illegal migrants not only exacerbates the border crisis but also represents a betrayal of the American people. It is high time for decisive action to secure our borders, uphold the rule of law, and protect the interests of American citizens. Anything less would be a dereliction of duty and a grave disservice to the nation.

FACING REALITY:

BIDEN ADMINISTRATION ACKNOWLEDGES SOUTHERN BORDER CRISIS

The Biden administration has finally conceded what conservatives and border security experts have long recognized: the situation at the southern border is undeniably a crisis. After years of downplaying the severity of the influx of migrants crossing illegally, the White House has abandoned its previous reluctance to use the term "crisis" and now acknowledges the urgent need for action. The shift in language was underscored by White House spokesman John Kirby's admission that "there is a crisis going on at the border." This marked departure from previous messaging, where the administration sought to characterize the historic surge in illegal border crossings as merely a "challenge."

President Biden himself reinforced this acknowledgment, stating that his administration had been "negotiating" with Congress for "two months" to address the border crisis. Furthermore, the president vowed to take decisive action, declaring that he would "shut down the border right now" if granted new powers by Congress.

This admission of the border crisis is not only a recognition of reality but also a tacit acknowledgment of the failure of the administration's immigration policies. The unprecedented surge in illegal border crossings, fueled by lax enforcement and misguided policies, has overwhelmed border communities, strained law enforcement resources, and fueled humanitarian concerns.

The consequences of the border crisis extend far beyond the border region, impacting communities across the nation and undermining the integrity of the immigration system. The Biden administration's refusal to address the root causes of illegal immigration, coupled with its rhetoric of open borders and leniency, has only exacerbated the situation, emboldening traffickers and incentivizing further illegal entry.

As Americans, we have long warned of the dangers of unchecked illegal immigration and advocated for commonsense border security measures to protect American sovereignty and national security. The Biden administration's belated recognition of the border crisis is a step in the right direction, but words alone are not enough.

Action must follow rhetoric, and meaningful reforms are needed to secure the border, enforce immigration laws, and safeguard the interests of American citizens.

Now is the time for bold leadership and decisive action to address the root causes of illegal immigration, strengthen border security, and restore order to our immigration system. The Biden administration must prioritize the safety and security of the American people above all else and work in collaboration with Congress to enact meaningful reforms that address the ongoing crisis at our southern border. Anything less would be a betrayal of the trust placed in our elected leaders and a disservice to the nation as a whole.

America is facing a crisis at its southern border. After three years of evasion and denial, Biden's admission is a long overdue recognition of the catastrophic situation unfolding at the border. House Speaker Mike Johnson wasted no time in highlighting the gravity of the situation, aptly branding it not just a crisis, but a full-blown catastrophe.

The Biden administration's feeble attempts to shift blame and evade responsibility have been laid bare. Despite acknowledging the crisis, Biden continues to claim impotence in addressing the disaster he has wrought.

This assertion is not only disingenuous but outright false. The president possesses ample executive authority to take decisive action and stem the tide of illegal immigration. It is high time for him to abandon the excuse of executive incapacity and take meaningful steps to address the border crisis.

House Republicans have welcomed Biden's belated recognition of reality. However, their support does not extend to the border deal currently being negotiated in the Senate. Many Republicans vehemently oppose the proposed deal, arguing that it would only exacerbate the crisis by facilitating as many as 150,000 illegal crossings monthly. Despite reassurances from supporters of the deal, skeptics remain unconvinced of its efficacy.

Oklahoma Sen. James Lankford, the leading Republican negotiator, has emerged as a vocal critic of the proposed compromise. He has labeled it as "the most conservative border security bill in four decades," a dubious distinction that fails to assuage concerns about its potential consequences. Lankford's opposition underscores the deep divisions within Congress over how best to address the border crisis and secure America's sovereignty.

As Americans, we cannot afford to ignore the catastrophic implications of Biden's border policies. The unchecked influx of illegal immigrants poses a grave threat to national security, public safety, and the integrity of our immigration system. It is imperative that we hold the Biden administration accountable for its failure to secure the border and protect the interests of the American people.

America grapples with a burgeoning border crisis, President Biden finds himself walking a precarious political tightrope, daring Republicans to reject proposed deals while attempting to deflect blame onto Congress. Yet, despite the administration's attempts to downplay the severity of the situation, recent developments have thrust the border crisis into the spotlight, prompting a sudden shift in rhetoric from the White House.

In a stunning display of political gymnastics, President Biden initially denied the existence of a crisis at the southern border, only to backtrack less than two weeks later as record-breaking encounters with migrants surged. The sudden change in language reflects the stark reality on the ground, with December alone witnessing a staggering 302,034 encounters, bringing the total for 2023 to a staggering 2.47 million – numbers that cannot be dismissed as anything but a crisis.

The Biden administration's attempts to spin the narrative have been met with skepticism, particularly in light of recent statements from Department of Homeland Security Secretary Alejandro Mayorkas. Despite overwhelming evidence to the contrary, Mayorkas adamantly refused to label the situation as a crisis, instead characterizing it as a mere "challenge" that the administration is purportedly addressing with vigor.

This semantic dance is more than a matter of semantics – it speaks to a broader reluctance within the administration to confront the gravity of the situation head-on. Mayorkas's refusal to utter the word "crisis" is emblematic of an administration seemingly more concerned with optics than with addressing the root causes of the border surge. By shying away from acknowledging the crisis, the administration risks further eroding public trust and exacerbating the humanitarian and security challenges posed by unchecked immigration.

As Americans, we refuse to be gaslit by the Biden administration's attempts to downplay the border crisis. The influx of illegal immigrants poses a clear and present danger to national security, public safety, and the integrity of our immigration system. It is incumbent upon President Biden and Congress to prioritize border security and enact meaningful reforms to address the root causes of illegal immigration.

In the face of mounting challenges at the border crisis, We Christian Conservative Americans are urging steadfastness and resolve in the pursuit of effective border security measures. Despite President Biden's recent policy shifts and rhetoric, concerns persist over the administration's handling of illegal immigration and its impact on national security and sovereignty.

As the number of encounters at the southern border continues to rise, President Biden has attempted to downplay the severity of the situation, attributing the surge to longstanding issues rather than his administration's policies. However, the reality on the ground tells a different story, prompting calls for a more muscular response to illegal immigration.

The proposed border deal, supported by Senate Republicans, offers a glimmer of hope for a stronger stance on border security. Advocates argue that the legislation would provide much-needed reinforcements to stem the tide of illegal crossings and safeguard America's borders. Yet, the likelihood of Congress sending such legislation to Biden's desk appears increasingly uncertain, raising concerns among Conservative Christians and majority of Americans about the administration's commitment to protecting the nation's borders.

President Biden's policy reversals, including the repeal of former President Trump's "remain in Mexico" policy and the halting of border wall construction, have only exacerbated tensions at the border. The recent standoff with Texas over the erection of razor wire along the Rio Grande underscores the deep divide over immigration policy and enforcement.

Furthermore, the administration's reluctance to acknowledge the border crisis has raised eyebrows among Christian nationalists, who view the situation as a clear and present danger to the nation's security and well-being. While Biden has previously described the border as a "crisis," his subsequent attempts to downplay the severity of the situation have only fueled skepticism about his administration's priorities and commitment to enforcing immigration laws.

The time for political gamesmanship is over. President Biden must set aside partisan politics and work with Republicans to implement policies that secure the border, enforce immigration laws, and protect the interests of the American people. Anything less would be a dereliction of duty and a betrayal of the trust placed in him by the American people.

In the face of these challenges, Majority of Americans are calling for unwavering resolve and principled leadership in addressing the border crisis. They reject attempts to obscure the truth and demand action to secure America's borders and uphold the rule of law. As the debate over immigration policy continues to unfold, Christian American nationalists stand firm in their commitment to defending the nation's sovereignty and security, ensuring a safer and more prosperous future for all Americans.

INSIDE THE MIND OF
THE PRESIDENT:

Upholding Transparency or Weaponizing Information
THE CASE OF BIDEN'S MEMORY LAPSES

In recent days, the corridors of political discourse have been abuzz with the aftermath of Special Counsel Robert Hur's decision to delve into the mental acuity of President Joe Biden during a federal investigation. The Biden administration, flanked by legal analysts from liberal news networks, has vehemently criticized Hur's inclusion of the president's memory lapses and age in his deposition, citing it as inappropriate and damaging.

However, amidst the cacophony of dissent, Andrew McCarthy, a seasoned editor at the National Review, has stood firm in defense of Hur's actions. McCarthy contends that Hur's mention of Biden's memory lapses was not merely permissible but necessary in the pursuit of transparency and accountability. He argues that failing to address concerns regarding the president's mental health could have far-reaching implications, potentially even warranting the invocation of the 25th Amendment.

In closing, McCarthy's defense of Hur's actions serves as a reminder of the complex interplay between transparency, accountability, and individual privacy in the realm of federal investigations. While critics may decry Hur's decision as a breach of protocol, McCarthy offers a compelling argument for the necessity of confronting uncomfortable truths, even at the highest levels of government. As the debate rages on, one thing remains clear: in the pursuit of justice, no stone can be left unturned, even if it means confronting uncomfortable realities about those in power.

The Biden White House is a trainwreck when it comes to handling accountability and justice. The findings of a federal investigation into Biden's actions have been shamelessly brushed aside, with the administration opting to label them as nothing more than a partisan attack. But the truth is glaringly obvious: Biden's age and mental acuity are not excuses for willfully retaining classified information.

The Biden White House is a trainwreck when it comes to handling accountability and justice. The findings of a federal investigation into Biden's actions have been shamelessly brushed aside, with the administration opting to label them as nothing more than a partisan attack. But the truth is glaringly obvious: Biden's age and mental acuity are not excuses for willfully retaining classified information.

The dismissive attitude displayed by the Biden camp is unfortunately not surprising. It seems to be the default reaction of Democrats whenever they find themselves in hot water. But this time, it's particularly egregious. The president of the United States has been found to have knowingly kept classified information, yet he's somehow deemed too senile to face charges. This is a clear example of the two systems of justice at work—one for Biden and another for his predecessor, President Trump.

But the injustice doesn't end there. Another layer of corruption emerges with the case of Biden's ghostwriter, Mark Zwonitzer. Zwonitzer was not charged with obstruction despite deleting audio tapes related to the president's second book, "Promise Me, Dad," upon learning they were under federal investigation. Biden reportedly disclosed classified information on these tapes to Zwonitzer, yet the writer faced no consequences.

In contrast, under the Trump administration, two staffers were charged for merely moving some boxes. The glaring disparity in treatment is evident for all to see. While Zwonitzer provided what authorities deemed "plausible, innocent reasons" for his actions, Trump's associates were not afforded the same leniency.

The Biden administration's handling of these matters underscores a troubling trend—one where accountability is selectively applied depending on political affiliation. It's a disservice to the principles of justice and fairness that our nation purports to uphold. If we are to truly uphold the rule of law, then it must apply equally to all, regardless of their position or political persuasion.

The Biden White House's response to the special counsel report on the mishandling of classified information is nothing short of a trainwreck. The blatant disregard for accountability and justice is alarming and sets a dangerous precedent for future administrations.

It's time for the American people to demand transparency and accountability from those in power, regardless of their political affiliation. Anything less is a betrayal of our democratic principles.

Paul Begala, a prominent figure on CNN and a staunch advocate for the Democratic Party, has found himself in an unenviable position. Even with his well-documented loyalty to the Democratic cause, Begala cannot spin the damning contents of Special Counsel Robert Hur's report regarding Joe Biden's egregious mishandling of classified information. The report, which has surfaced recently, paints a grim picture of Biden's actions, leaving little room for excuses or evasion.

Hur's report, according to Begala's own admission, lays bare a series of troubling revelations. Biden is implicated in willfully retaining classified materials, sharing sensitive information with unauthorized individuals, notably his ghostwriter, and displaying a concerning degradation in mental capacity during his interview with investigators. The latter point is particularly unsettling, indicating a significant decline in Biden's cognitive faculties that raises serious questions about his fitness for office.

Begala's reaction to the report is telling. He reportedly expressed a sense of relief, claiming to have slept like a baby, albeit for only two hours and accompanied by bedwetting. Such a reaction underscores the magnitude of the disaster this report represents for the Democratic Party. It serves as a stark reminder of the ethical and moral responsibilities entrusted to those in positions of power, responsibilities that must never be overshadowed by partisan allegiances or political expediency.

The implications of the Hur report extend far beyond mere political ramifications. They strike at the heart of the integrity of our nation's leadership and the fundamental principles upon which our democracy is built. The mishandling of classified information, especially by those entrusted with the highest levels of authority, cannot and must not be tolerated.

As a Journalist, it is our duty to hold those in power accountable, regardless of their political affiliation. The revelations contained within the Hur report demand a thorough and impartial investigation, followed by appropriate measures to ensure that such egregious breaches of trust never occur again.

The findings of Special Counsel Robert Hur's report regarding Joe Biden's mishandling of classified information are deeply troubling and demand serious attention. Even staunch Democratic loyalists like Paul Begala cannot spin the gravity of these revelations. It is imperative that we uphold the principles of accountability and integrity in our political system, irrespective of partisan interests. The American people deserve nothing less.

President Joe Biden's cognitive lapses, a specter of doubt looms over the Oval Office. While the immediate threat of indictment may have dissipated, the contents of the report have resurrected long-standing questions regarding Biden's fitness to hold the highest office in the land. This isn't merely partisan nitpicking; it's a legitimate concern for the stability and efficacy of United States government.

Joe Biden presidential portrait Photo by Adam Schultz

President Joe Biden's cognitive lapses, a specter of doubt looms over the Oval Office. While the immediate threat of indictment may have dissipated, the contents of the report have resurrected long-standing questions regarding Biden's fitness to hold the highest office in the land. This isn't merely partisan nitpicking; it's a legitimate concern for the stability and efficacy of United States government.

The incident involving Biden's erroneous claims of conversations with deceased world leaders underscores a troubling pattern that has persisted throughout his presidency. Whether it's forgetfulness on the campaign trail or confusion during official duties, the narrative of Biden's mental acuity continues to haunt the public consciousness.

It's no secret that age catches up with us all, and Biden is no exception. Despite attempts to downplay his cognitive decline, the stark reality remains: the presidency demands sharpness of mind and clarity of thought, qualities that seem increasingly elusive for the current occupant of the White House.

What's perhaps most concerning is the manner in which the Biden administration has responded to these challenges. Instead of addressing legitimate concerns head-on, they have resorted to evasion and deflection. The "basement strategy" of minimizing Biden's public appearances may have served as a temporary reprieve, but it's become increasingly untenable in the face of mounting scrutiny.

Last night's fiasco, where Biden stumbled over basic details like the name of a church or the leaders of key nations, only underscores the urgency of the situation. The American people deserve a leader who can inspire confidence and command respect, not one who struggles to recall basic facts or mangles crucial details in international affairs.

For Democrats, the dilemma is clear: they can no longer afford to ignore the elephant in the room. The prospect of putting Biden on the public stage more frequently is fraught with risk, as each stumble further erodes his credibility and raises doubts about his ability to govern effectively.

In the end, this isn't about partisan politics or scoring political points. It's about ensuring the stability and integrity of our democracy. If Biden's cognitive decline continues unchecked, the consequences could be dire not just for his presidency, but for the nation as a whole. It's time for Democrats to confront this uncomfortable truth and consider the long-term implications for United States future.

VOTE
2024
SUPREME
COURT SIGNALS
POTENTIAL VICTORY FOR TRUMP
IN BALLOT ELIGIBILITY CASE

In a significant legal showdown, the U.S. Supreme Court heard arguments on whether former President Donald Trump should be allowed on the ballot for the upcoming November election. The case revolves around Colorado's decision to disqualify Trump based on allegations that he engaged in insurrection at the U.S. Capitol.

During the hearing, the justices displayed scepticism towards Colorado's stance and posed tough questions to the state's lawyer. The top court in Colorado had previously ruled that Trump was ineligible to be on the ballot due to his alleged involvement in the Capitol insurrection.

However, Thursday's 8th Feb 2024 proceedings suggested that the Supreme Court may lean towards supporting the 45th president's appeal.

Speaking to reporters outside his Mar-a-Lago estate, Trump characterized the Supreme Court hearing as "a very beautiful process." He expressed hope that democracy would prevail, underscoring the significance of the ongoing legal battle for his political future.

The Supreme Court justices' tough questioning of Colorado's decision signals a potential shift in favor of Trump, raising questions about the validity of the initial disqualification ruling. Critics argue that the case could set a precedent for how states handle the eligibility of candidates with controversial backgrounds.

Trump's assertion that the hearing was a "very beautiful process" reflects his optimism about the legal proceedings and his confidence in the justice system. The former president emphasized his commitment to the democratic process, reinforcing the idea that he sees the court's intervention as crucial to upholding democratic values.

Former President Donald Trump's recent statement regarding the Supreme Court hearing on February 8, 2024, underscores the urgent need to safeguard democracy against the onslaught of radical left ideas and the weaponization of politics. In his remarks, Trump highlighted the concerning trend of using political power to manipulate legal processes and undermine electoral integrity.

Trump's characterization of the Supreme Court proceedings as a "very beautiful process" reflects his appreciation for the fundamental principles of justice and the rule of law. Despite facing relentless attacks and baseless allegations, Trump maintains his faith in the American judicial system and its ability to uphold democratic values.

The former president's concerns about the weaponization of politics ring true in the current political climate, where partisan agendas often take precedence over the rule of law. Trump's assertion that these tactics are "totally illegal" underscores the gravity of the situation and the need for decisive action to protect the integrity of the electoral process.

Trump's reference to specific cases, such as the one in Georgia involving allegations of election interference, sheds light on the disturbing pattern of collusion between partisan actors and government institutions. The revelation of staged meetings and coordinated efforts to undermine the electoral process is deeply troubling and demands accountability.

Moreover, Trump's condemnation of election interference emanating from the White House and the Biden administration highlights the need for transparency and accountability in government. The sanctity of the electoral process must be upheld, free from undue influence and partisan manipulation.

Trump's call for the dismissal of frivolous lawsuits and baseless accusations serves as a reminder of the importance of due process and the rule of law. In a democracy, every citizen is entitled to a fair and impartial legal proceeding, free from political bias or ulterior motives.

As Trump rightly points out, the millions of Americans who support him and the Republican Party deserve to have their voices heard without fear of manipulation or interference. The outcome of the Supreme Court hearing must reflect the will of the people and uphold the principles of democracy that have guided this nation for centuries.

Former President Donald Trump didn't hold back in his scathing assessment of President Joe Biden's administration, labeling it as "the worst in the history of our country" and criticizing Biden's ability to articulate coherent thoughts.

Trump lambasted Biden's handling of various crises, attributing them to the outcome of the 2020 election. Trump pointed to the ongoing Ukrainian conflict with Russia, the attack on Israel, rising inflation, tensions with China over Taiwan, and the enrichment of Iran as consequences of Biden's presidency.

Highlighting his own administration's accomplishments, Trump said credit for leaving Iran economically weakened and unable to support terrorist organizations like Hamas and Hezbollah. He expressed concern over Iran's newfound financial strength, which he believes poses a significant threat to regional stability.

Trump also warned of the looming specter of a potential World War III under Biden's leadership, questioning his ability to negotiate effectively with global adversaries like Vladimir Putin, Xi Jinping, and Kim Jong-un. Trump

criticized Biden's reliance on military intervention, arguing that it only exacerbates conflicts and wastes taxpayer money.

Furthermore, Trump lamented the deteriorating situation in the Middle East, citing escalating violence and unnecessary loss of life. He reiterated his belief in the principle of "peace through strength" and criticized Biden's perceived lack of strategic foresight in managing international crises.

The former president's scathing critique underscores the deep partisan divide in American politics, with conservatives increasingly vocal in their opposition to the Biden administration's policies and actions. Trump's remarks are likely to resonate with his supporters, who continue to view his presidency as a period of stability and progress for the nation.

EXCLUSIVE INVITATION

The Honor of Your Presence is Requested at a

BORDER911 Gala

501(C)(3) Foundation

The **Mar-a-Lago** Club

Poolside Reception

Formal Gala Dinner in Ballroom

Dignitaries, Members
of Congress and Celebrities

Kash Patel

Sebastian Gorka
EMCEE

The Honorable

Tom Homan

Former ICE Director to the 45th President, Donald J. Trump

BORDER 911 Team

Sara Carter | Mark Morgan | Derek Maltz | Rodney Scott | Jaeson Jones

Host Committee

Matt Whitaker | Anthony Marlowe | Steve Moore | Sam Sorbo
Kevin Sorbo | Monica Crowley | Joe Piscopo | Congressman Ronny Jackson

April 4, 2024

BORDER911.com/events/

6:00PM - Poolside Reception
7:30PM - Ballroom Gala
Black Tie

Do Not Miss This Historic Once In A Lifetime Extravaganza!

Poolside Reception $ 900
Gala and Reception $ 2,500
Maga Patriot $ 10,000
(Private round table with celebrity)

Ambassador $ 5,000
**(Includes Red Carpet Pictures
and VIP seating)**

Sponsor $ 100,000

Text: Martha 571 839 1143

Donations submitted through donation
forms on this site are tax-deductible to the
extent allowed by law and are proccessed in
U.S. dollars. BORDER911 Foundation, Inc. is a
U.S. nonprofit, tax-exempt charitable
organization (Tax Identification Number 93-
3033002) under Section 501(c)(3) of the U.S.
Internal Revenue Code.

www.ingramcontent.com/pod-product-compliance
Lightning Source LLC
Chambersburg PA
CBHW080922160726
48000CB00009B/3095